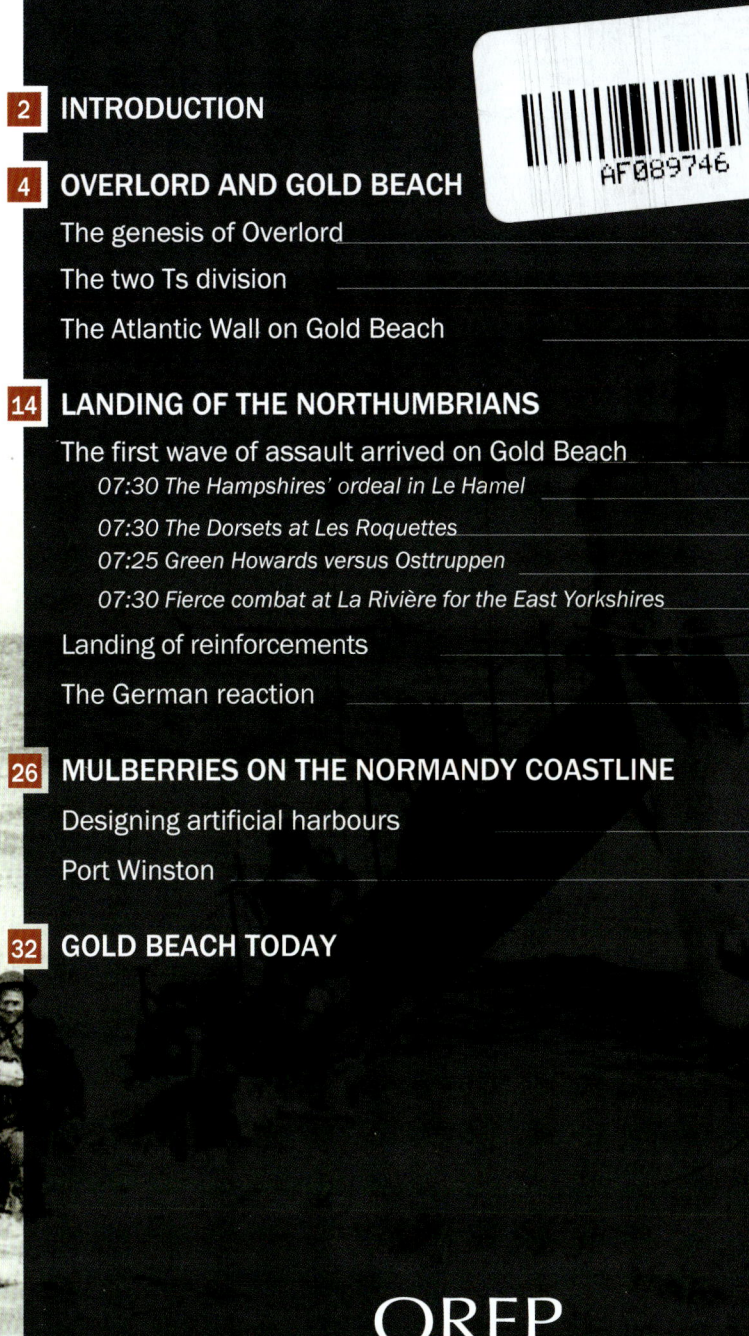

2 INTRODUCTION

4 OVERLORD AND GOLD BEACH

The genesis of Overlord — 4
The two Ts division — 6
The Atlantic Wall on Gold Beach — 10

14 LANDING OF THE NORTHUMBRIANS

The first wave of assault arrived on Gold Beach — 17
   07:30 The Hampshires' ordeal in Le Hamel — 17
   07:30 The Dorsets at Les Roquettes — 18
   07:25 Green Howards versus Osttruppen — 19
   07:30 Fierce combat at La Rivière for the East Yorkshires — 20
Landing of reinforcements — 21
The German reaction — 24

26 MULBERRIES ON THE NORMANDY COASTLINE

Designing artificial harbours — 26
Port Winston — 29

32 GOLD BEACH TODAY

OREP
EDITIONS

Zone tertiaire de Nonant 14400 BAYEUX
Tél: 02 31 51 81 31 - Fax: 02 31 51 81 32
info@orepeditions.com - **www.orepeditions.com**

Editor: Grégory Pique
Editorial coordinator: Corine Desprez
English Translation: Heather Costil

Graphic design : OREP
ISBN: 978-2-8151-0723-5 - © Éditions OREP 2023
All rights reserved - Legal deposit: 2nd quarter 2012

GOLD BEACH

Battalions from the 151st Brigade landing in the King sector in the afternoon.

Two figures swam inconspicuously towards the Normandy coastline. Despite their kapok-lined rubber diving suits, both suffered from the severe cold. For temperatures were close to zero on this New Year's night. After a speed boat brought them from Great Britain, Major Scott-Bowden from the Royal Engineers and Sergeant Ogden-Smith finally climbed aboard small canoes before swimming the last 200 yards of their Channel crossing to the shore. They advanced across the sandy beach, all senses on the alert. The lighthouse at Ver-sur-Mer cast an intermittent beam across the entire beach, obliging them to progress with great caution.

Doing their utmost to attract no attention, the two men collected samples of sand and peat from various locations. They could hear the distant sound of festivities. The Germans were busy celebrating the New Year. The two British soldiers rapidly completed their mission and returned to the shoreline. They tried to swim back out to sea, but the waves were too high. So they waited, and they watched the ebb and flow, before finally swimming away from the beach.

Out at sea, Scott-Bowden suddenly heard what he thought to be a cry for help from his buddy. As he approached, he realized that Ogden-Smith was in fact wishing him a Happy New Year. They were just a few minutes into 1944 and five months later some 25,000 troops were to set foot on the very same beach: Gold Beach.

OVERLORD AND GOLD BEACH

THE GENESIS OF OVERLORD

Scott-Bowden and Ogden-Smith's mission was but one of a multitude of tasks accomplished by the Allies with the aim of establishing a foothold in France. Several operations of varying types were led, akin to the one to collect samples of sand for analysis in order to determine whether landing vehicles would run the risk of sinking into it as soon as they arrived on the beach.

The British Prime Minister, Winston Churchill, was keen to return to the Continent since the 1940 retreat from Dunkirk. Yet, his German enemy was still too powerful and only small-scale operations - commando missions - were feasible. Lord Mountbatten was therefore entrusted with the command of Combined Operations in 1941 and thanks to his small commando units, he plagued the German forces from Spitzbergen to the Bay of Biscay.

LCT Landing Craft Tank landing barges on the Southampton docks. The date for the landing operation had been postponed in order to accumulate sufficient numbers of these precious vessels. IWM A023730.

When the United States entered the war in December 1941, the order of things changed irretrievably. Although the American military power was still in its infancy, the event was to lead Churchill to pronounce these famous words, «We have won the war». A succession of conferences were organised between the two Allied nations to develop a common strategy.

The first, held just three weeks later in Washington, defined Germany as the Allies' principal enemy. Hence the «Germany first» strategy. However, in order to overwhelm the Nazi regime, troops, tanks, planes and transport ships needed to be dispatched across the Atlantic (the Bolero plan). Then began a fierce battle with Admiral Dönitz' packs of U-Boote which incessantly stalked the Allied convoys. In 1943, thanks to major advances in underwater operations, the Allies were to win this battle of the Atlantic.

Canadian propaganda poster. Indeed, 1944 was a decisive year for the war, with the success of the Allied D-Day landings to the west and the arrival of Soviet troops on the frontiers of the Reich.

In 1942, Churchill and the American President Roosevelt came to a deadlock over the best strategy to adopt. The Americans were clearly in favour of a direct attack on the enemy via a landing operation in France. Several battle plans were consequently developed: Round up and Sledgehammer. Yet the British were highly sceptical on the chances of success of such an operation. They believed that the armed forces being grouped together in Great Britain were, as yet, insufficient to break through the Atlantic Wall. They were more readily in favour of peripheral operations, in particular in the Mediterranean, likely to facilitate overpowering the Reich from the south. It was Churchill's view that initially prevailed the American and British troops landed in North Africa in November 1942. They subsequently ousted the Axis powers from Tunisia in May 1943 before moving on to Sicily and southern Italy, where they came to a standstill before Rome on the Gustav line.

British propaganda poster illustrating Churchill's «bulldog» tenacity. The British Prime Minister was behind the creation of the commando units who relentlessly intimidated the German defences as from 1940.

Despite dissension between the Allied forces, an inter-Allied committee, the COSSAC (Chief of Staff to the Supreme Allied Commander), commanded by General Morgan, was formed in April 1943. The committee was entrusted with the mission of establishing the plans for a cross Channel invasion, soon to be baptised Overlord. The essential remaining questions were where and when. The COSSAC's plan was approved at the Quebec Conference, codenamed Quadrant, held in August: the landing would take place in Normandy, in May 1944.

THE TWO TS DIVISION

A Supreme Commander was appointed in December 1943: General Eisenhower, who had already demonstrated his great qualities as an organiser and diplomat in Africa and Italy. With support from the British General Montgomery, in charge of land forces, he established the final plans for Overlord: three airborne divisions were to be dropped by night to cover the flanks of the invasion zone then, at dawn, five divisions were to land between the eastern base of the Cotentin peninsula and the Orne estuary, on five beaches codenamed Utah and Omaha in the American sector and Gold, Juno and Sword in the Anglo-Canadian sector.

50th Northumbrian Infantry Division insignia.

In October 1943, the mission to land on Gold Beach was entrusted to General Douglas Graham's 50th Northumbrian Infantry Division, an experienced division engaged in combat since the very first hours of the conflict. The unit essentially comprised territorial battalions from the counties of Northumberland and Durham, in the regions around Newcastle and Middlesbrough, in northwest England. Its insignia, comprising two superimposed 'T's that combine to form an 'H' represents the three rivers that run through these counties, the Tyne, the Tees and the Humber.

In May 1940, the division fought in the Battle of Arras, counter-attacking the tanks from Field Marshal Rommel's 7. Panzerdivision. It then withdrew towards Dunkirk and boarded for England, leaving behind its heavy equipment on the beach. The division was later dispatched to Africa, where it distinguished itself during the Battles of Gazala (May 1942) and El Alamein (October - November 1942). After the Axis powers had surrendered in Tunisia, the division moved to Sicily on the 10th of July 1943, and advanced towards Messina. The Normandy landings were, therefore, far from the first amphibious operation for the division's veterans. Finally, in October of the same year, the division was sent the Great Britain to train for Overlord.

▲ The 50th Division was an experienced unit with specific expertise in amphibious operations. Men from the Northumbrian fighting in the streets of Acireale in August 1943 after landing on the Sicilian coast for Operation Husky. IWM NA005845

The SHAEF (Supreme Headquarters Allied Expeditionary Force) - the entire inter-Allied staff - from left to right: General Bradley, Commander of the US First Army, Admiral Ramsay, Naval Force Commander, Air Marshal Tedder, Second in Command, General Eisenhower, Supreme Commander, General Montgomery, Commander of ground forces, his compatriot Leigh Mallory, Air Commander and General Bedell-Smith, Chief of Staff.

OVERLORD AND GOLD BEACH

Major General Graham took command of the division on the 19th of January 1944. The unit was then to be submitted to intensive training in Hampshire, during which it took part in amphibious operations aimed at testing and improving landing techniques. On D-Day, the division covered the Anglo-Canadian left flank, with support from powerful reinforcements. Over and above the two extra artillery regiments, an independent infantry brigade, the 56th Brigade, also joined the division. Further support was offered by the 8th Armoured Brigade and the 47th Royal Marine commando unit came to complete the assault force. Special tanks were brought in from the 79th Armoured Division. Major General Graham's mission was to weaken the German defences between Asnelles and Ver-sur-Mer before liberating Bayeux. He was also to link with the American troops who were to land westwards on Omaha Beach and with the Canadians arriving from the east, on Juno Beach.

50th Northumbrian Infantry Division
(Major General Graham) 25,000 men

231st Brigade
(Brig. Stanier)
1st wave of assault

69th Brigade
(Brig. Knox)
1st wave of assault

Divisional Units

1st Btn, The Hampshire Regiment
(Lt Col Nelson-Smith)

1st Btn, The Dorsetshire Regiment
(Lt Col Norie)

2nd Btn, The Devonshire Regiment (support)
(Lt Col Nevill)

5th Btn, The East Yorkshire Regiment
(Lt Col White)

6th Btn, The Green Howards
(Lt Col Hastings)

7th Btn, The Green Howards (support)
(Lt Col Richardson)

5 artillery groups
74th Field Regiment RA
86th Field regiment RA
90th Field Regiment RA
124th Field Regiment RA
147th Field Regiment RA
(120 x 105mm SP Guns, Priest)

1 anti-tank group
102nd Anti-Tank Regiment RA
(48 x 17 pounders)

1 anti-aircraft group
25th Light Anti-Aircraft Regiment RA
(54 x Bofors 40mm guns)

1 machine gun battalion
2nd Btn, The Cheshire Regiment MG

1 reconnaissance unit
61st Recce Regiment

Men from the 50th Division preparing the landings on Gold Beach.

50th Northumbrian Infantry Division
(Major General Graham) 25,000 men

56th Brigade
(Brig. Pepper) Independent reinforcement brigade

2nd Btn, The South Wales Borderers
(Lt Col Craddock)

2nd Btn, The Gloucestershire Regiment
(Lt Col Biddle)

2nd Btn, The Essex Regiment
(Lt Col Higson)

151st Brigade
(Brig. Senior) Reinforcement brigade

6th Btn, The Durham Light Infantry
(Lt Col Green)

8th Btn, The Durham Light Infantry
(Lt Col Lidwill)

9th Btn, The Durham Light Infantry
(Lt Col Woods)

Attached unit
British 8th Armoured Brigade
(Brig. Cracroft)

The Nottinghamshire Yeomanry
or
Sherwood Rangers
(Lt Col Anderson)

4th/7th Dragoon Guards
(Lt Col Byron)

24th Lancers
(Lt Col Anderson)

12th Kings Royal Rifle Corps
(Lt Col Oxley)

Other attached units

47th Royal Marine Commando (Lt Col Phillips)
Crab anti-mine tanks: **Westminster Dragoons B and C Squadrons**

Other special tanks:
81st and 82nd Squadrons from the 6th Assault Regiment, Royal Engineers

Major General Douglas Graham

Douglas Graham was born in Scotland in 1893. This somewhat austere figure was a First World War veteran. During the Second World War, he was first sent to Palestine, then to North Africa where he commanded a brigade. He was promoted to the grade of Major General in 1942 and took command of the 56th London Infantry Division with which he took part in the difficult landing in Salerno, to the south of Naples. He was wounded during the operation and was sent back to Britain to recover. In January 1944, given his extensive experience in amphibious operations, he was entrusted with the command of the 50th Infantry Division that was to land on Gold Beach He remained in command of the division until the end of the war. He retired in 1947 and died in 1971.

▲ General Graham, Commander of the 50th Division, in conversation with General Montgomery. The unit's insignia can clearly be seen on Graham's shoulder. *IWM B005787.*

The division left its camp on the 3rd of June to board the Force G vessels berthed in Southampton and Portsmouth. However, poor weather loomed over the English Channel and Eisenhower finally decided to postpone the operation 24 hours. D-Day was consequently rescheduled for Tuesday the 6th of June. When Commodore Douglas-Pennant's Force G ships reached the other convoys in the high seas off the Isle of Wight on the morning of the 5th of June, force 4 winds and 6-feet-high waves awaited them. On board, the men from the 50th Division were already battling - with sea sickness.

THE ATLANTIC WALL ON GOLD BEACH

Scott-Bowden and Ogden-Smith were aware that the zone that was to become Gold Beach was already under strict German surveillance by the end of 1943; the previous year, Hitler had ordered the construction of the famous Atlantic Wall by the Organisation Todt. Although it was far from the formidable barrier described by German propaganda, it was nevertheless an obstacle that the Allies could not afford to neglect. The decision to land in Normandy was also the consequence of the extensive fortification by the Germans of the Pas-de-Calais coast which they considered to be the most likely site for a landing operation.

A Landing Ship Tank (LST) approaching the Normandy coast. Capable of transporting 300 men and 60 tanks, these flat-hulled vessels equipped with bow doors could ground directly on the beach to land their vehicles.

When, in November 1943, Field Marshal Rommel was appointed inspector of fortifications in the West, he was appalled by the lack of progression of construction work in certain sectors. He subsequently devoted all of his efforts and resourcefulness into perfecting German defences, from Denmark to the Pyrenees.

On D-Day, the Allies would need to challenge three successive defensive lines. First of all, on the beaches, series of traps and obstacles had been installed to prevent landing barges from approaching the shoreline. Tetrahedrons, Czech hedgehogs, mined stakes, Belgian gates... were positioned in such a manner that the Allies would need to land at low tide, hence exposing their men to machine gunfire and mortar fire from the German defensive positions.

Atlantic Wall blockhouse construction site. The OrganisationTodt made vast use of local manpower.

For indeed, strong points had been established

here and there along the entire coast, each strong point covering its neighbours. These *Widerstandnesten* (WN) comprised machine guns and mortars, some of them housed in shelters, and a few bunkers to protect anti-tank guns.

Finally, the third line consisted of artillery batteries located further inland. Certain pieces of artillery were installed in the middle of fields, whilst others were genuine defensive complexes with guns housed in casemates; the artillery battery in Longues-sur-Mer is a fine example. Well before the landing operation, these positions had been the target of Allied bombers; however the vast majority of these concrete defences had withstood Allied attacks.

The defensive positions established on Gold Beach were as follows:

LOCATION	STRONG POINT	WEAPONS	COMPANY
Longues-sur-Mer Longues artillery battery	WN 48	4 x 150mm Czech guns	
Arromanches-les-Bains Le Petit Fontaine	WN 45	abandoned	2nd Company (726th Rgt)
Arromanches-les-Bains Tracy-sur-Mer	WN 44	1 x 47mm gun housed in a casemate	
Arromanches-les-Bains West of the village	WN 43	1 x 105mm gun housed in a casemate	
Arromanches-les-Bains East of the village	Stp 42	Radar station 1 x 75mm gun housed in a casemate 3 x 20mm anti-aircraft guns	1st Company (726th Rgt)
Arromanches-les-Bains Le Petit Fontaine	WN 41	abandoned	
Arromanches-les-Bains Le puits d'Hérode	WN 40	abandoned	
Saint-Côme-de-Fresné North of the village	WN 39	2 x 75mm guns housed in casemates	
Saint-Côme-de-Fresné East of the village	WN 38	2 x 50mm guns housed in casemates	

11

LOCATION	STRONG POINT	WEAPONS	COMPANY
Asnelles Le Hamel	WN 37	1 x 75mm gun housed in a casemate 1 x 50mm gun housed in a casemate	1st compagny (726th Rgt)
Asnelles Cabane des douanes	WN 36	1 x 50mm gun housed in a casemate	
Ver-sur-Mer Hable de Heurtot	WN 35		3rd compagny (441st Ost Btn)
Ver-sur-Mer Battery to the southwest	WN 35b	4 x 100mm guns	
Ver-sur-Mer Mont Fleury Battery	WN 35a	4 x 122mm guns housed in casemates	
Ver-sur-Mer Mont Fleury lighthouse	WN 34	1 x 50mm gun	7th compagny (736th Rgt)
Ver-sur-Mer La Rivière	WN 33	1 x 88mm gun housed in a casemate 2 x 50mm guns housed in casemates	
Ver-sur-Mer Mare-Fontaine Battery	WN 32	4 x 100mm guns housed in casemates	

OVERLORD AND GOLD BEACH

Vestiges of a concrete tetrahedron placed on the foreshore by the Germans in order to capsize or blow open landing barges arriving by high tide.

Remains of a casemate in the Mont Fleury artillery battery. This battery located to the north of Ver-sur-Mer was equipped with four seized Russian 122mm guns. Its construction was as yet incomplete at the time of the landings.

The entire sector from Port-en-Bessin to Ouistreham was defended by General Richter's *716.Infanterie-Division*. When the division was dispatched to the region of Caen in 1942, it comprised around seventeen thousand men. Yet the losses sustained on the Russian front obliged the Germans to tap into static divisions in order to reinforce the ranks in Russia. Shortly before the landings, Richter's unit had been reduced to but eight thousand soldiers. Most of them were tired veterans or foreign conscripts, referred to as *Osttruppen* (Eastern troops) - Soviet soldiers who had enlisted in the *Wehrmacht* to escape German prisons or the Gulag that awaited those who dared to oppose Stalin. The 441st *Osttruppen Battalion* was posted in Ver-sur-Mer and Asnelles.

Hence, Richter's severely diminished division was to face an assault by three reinforced infantry divisions and one airborne division. The balance of power was 5 to 1 in favour of the Allies. Apart from manning of the coastal defences, very few reserve units were available. Only a few units from the *Panzer Abteilung 200* belonging to the *21.Panzerdivision* could potentially intervene.

Field Marshal Rommel visiting one of his subordinates, Parachute Corps General Meindl. One endeavoured in vain to drive out the Allies, whilst the other resisted with his paratroops for several weeks in the Saint-Lô sector, before finally escaping the Falaise pocket.

British soldiers inspecting a blockhouse housing a 50mm gun. The thickest wall faced the sea in order to protect artillery pieces from Allied naval fire.

LANDING OF THE NORTHUMBRIANS

USS Arkansas, an American battleship opening fire on the morning of the 6th of June. Its mission was to reduce the German defences on Omaha Beach, also targeting the Longues artillery battery.

At 03:00 hours on the 6th of June 1944, the first Force G ships arrived off the shores of Gold Beach. This ninemile-long beach stretching from Port-en-Bessin to Ver-sur-Mer was divided into four sectors, codenamed: How, Item, Jig and King. The first two sectors were overlooked by a high cliff and were ill-suited for a landing operation. The British troops from the 231st Brigade consequently reached Gold Beach via the Jig sector, whereas the 69th Brigade landed in the King sector.

At 05:30 hours, Commodore Douglas Pennant's flagship, *HMS Bulolo*, anchored seven miles off the coastline. Whilst the German defences had already endured aerial bombardments throughout the night, the five cruisers and thirteen destroyers that formed Force K, the naval bombarding support force, opened fire on the German artillery batteries and strong points. Their targets had been established as follows:

SHIPS	PRINCIPAL WEAPONS	TARGET
HMS Orion	6 x 152mm guns	Mont Fleury battery
HMS Ajax	8 x 152mm guns	Longues-sur-Mer battery
HMS Argonaut	8 x 133mm guns	Vaux-sur-Aure battery
HMS Emerald	5 x 152mm guns	Puits d'Hérode battery
HNLMS Flores Dutch gunboat	3 x 150mm guns	Arromanches battery

The German artillery batteries retaliated but shyly to the Allied attack, with the exception of the Longues battery which forced the *Bulolo* to retreat from its anchorage point. The battery was finally neutralised.

Aerial view of the Longues battery taken on the 22nd of May 1944. Its four casemates were located inland, whereas a firing command post was positioned on the edge of the cliff. The

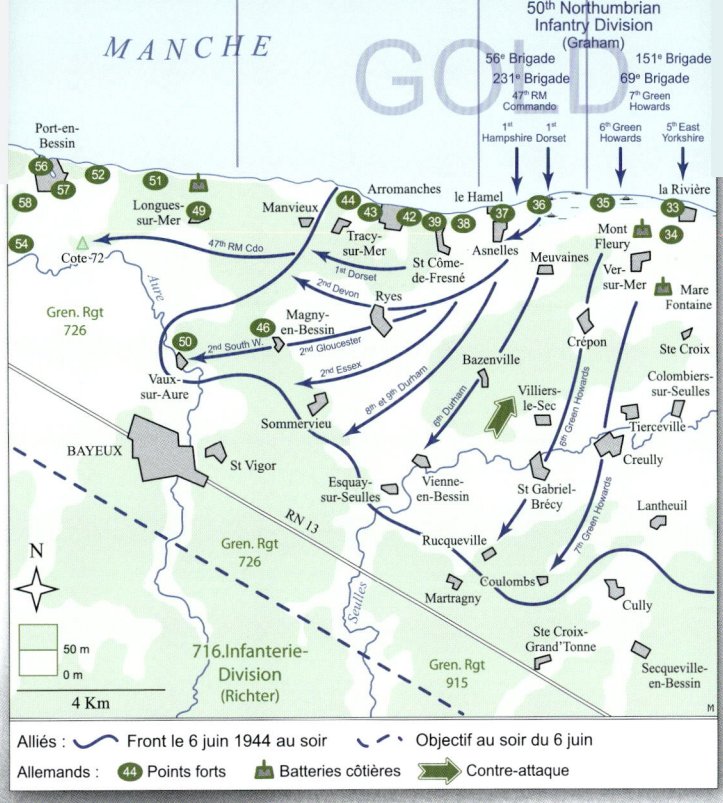

Concurrently, the troops left their LSI (Landing Ship Infantry) to board the LCA (Landing Craft Assault) landing barges that transported them over the remaining few miles that separated them from the Normandy shores.

Sherman Duplex Drive amphibious tanks equipped with inflatable skirts and a pair of propellers were to be launched 5,000 yards from the beach to arrive immediately before the infantry in order to neutralise the guns housed in casemates that comprised the German strong points. However, choppy seas were to postpone their landing. Most of them were either released closer to the shoreline or disembarked directly on the beach. They consequently landed simultaneously to the infantrymen which led to relative confusion. Confusion that was to be exacerbated by the fact that the special tanks equipped with an array of devices aimed at facilitating the operation also landed at the same time.

Plan of the British landings on Gold Beach.

Then at 07:30, the landing barge doors were lowered and the troops threw themselves into the water and headed for the beach.

A rarity: three of the four guns were left in place: 150mm Czechoslovakian guns taken from a torpedo boat. The fact that the Germans used various different types of artillery pieces was to generate major difficulties in ammunition supply.

The Longues-sur-Mer artillery battery

The battery in Longues-sur-Mer was armed with four 150mm Czech guns taken from a torpedo boat. They were all housed inside casemates. The firing command post was established on the cliffside and the position was protected by a series of shelters covered with barbed wire.

The battery suffered aerial bombing throughout the night then, at 05:37, the ships that had accompanied the troops who were to land on Omaha Beach opened fire. A long duel was to follow, opposing - on the Allied side - USS *Arkansas* and the French cruisers *Georges Leygues* and *Montcalm* and - on the German side - the Longues battery's four 150mm guns. The Force K ships positioned before Gold Beach, the cruiser *HMS Ajax* in particular, entered the battle at 06:00 hours. However, German gunfire forced Force G's flagship, the *Bulolo* to retreat from its point of anchor. Yet, combined attacks by *HMS Ajax* and *HMS Argonaut* were to finally neutralise three of the battery's four guns. Late in the afternoon, the last of its four guns resumed firing until 19:00 hours. It was only to be reduced to silence the following day, by the 2nd Devons.

▲The battery's four casemates are perfectly preserved. It remains a remarkable site for curious visitors keen to learn more about the Atlantic Wall blockhouses.

Picture taken at around 10:00 hours in Le Hamel, very probably of men from the *2nd Devons* as they progressed inland towards Ryes. They were covered by tanks from the 8th Armoured Brigade. ▶

THE FIRST WAVE OF ASSAULT ARRIVED ON GOLD BEACH

07:30 The Hampshires' ordeal in Le Hamel

Strong currents led the 1st Hampshires to drift eastwards and the battalion's first companies landed near Les Roquettes directly opposite the WN36 German strong point and under showers of deadly gunfire. The defensive position in Le Hamel, equipped with a 75mm gun, also destroyed several tanks. Nevertheless, the British troops finally managed to weave their way towards the road that ran parallel to the beach and headed for Le Hamel. Despite the arrival of the battalion's two other companies, strong point WN37 withstood all of the Allied assaults and retaliated at a cost of many lives. The battalion successively lost two of its commanders. Lieutenant-Colonel Nelson Smith was the first to be wounded and evacuated. Major Martin, who replaced him, was killed but a few moments later. To add to their misfortune, the observers who had been landed to assist in targeting naval artillery fire had also been wounded. Major Warren, who had taken command of the battalion, attempted attacks in various directions, but at midday Le Hamel was still in enemy hands and continued to hound the troops as they landed on the beach.

This blockhouse can still be seen today on the promenade in Asnelles. It housed a 75mm gun, protected by barbed wire mesh and a number of machine guns. WN37 was to give the men from the 1st Hampshires a very hard time throughout the entire day of the 6th of June.

07:30 The Dorsets at Les Roquettes

The 231st Brigade's other battalion, the 1st Dorsets, landed further eastwards at Les Roquettes. They were less exposed to gunfire from strong point WN36; however two Sherman DDs were destroyed and an anti-mine flail tank ended up exploding on one of them. Although three further special tanks were also lost, the battalion rapidly reassembled and the first sections headed for Le Buhot to the south of Asnelles.

A Westminster Dragoons flail tank, abandoned on the beach. The revolving drum at the front of the tank was equipped with chains which struck the ground, exploding land mines as it advanced. Yet the system was far from fail-safe since one of them ended up exploding on a mine on the Les Roquettes beach.

Lieutenant-Colonel Phillips' commandos arrived in the Jig sector as from 08:30. LCTs can be seen in the background unloading heavy equipment, in this case, special tanks to facilitate Engineer unit work.

LANDING OF THE NORTHUMBRIANS

07:25 Green Howards versus Osttruppen

With support from the Westminster Dragoons' special tanks, the 6th Green Howards were very quick to neutralise the strong point at Hable de Heurtot which was defended by an *Osttruppen* company. Yet, behind the beach, a vast marshy zone was to offer the British troops but one single route for their inland progression. Once beyond the marshland, the battalion headed for the Mont Fleury artillery battery to the northwest of Ver-sur-Mer. The position put up very little resistance for its servers had suffered heavy fire from the cruiser *HMS Orion*. At 09:30, the Green Howards assembled on the Meuvaines crest before heading for the village of Crépon.

Civilians tasting 50th Division rations in Ver-sur-Mer. The French people discovered products from the New World, such as chewing gum and corned beef.

Troops continued to arrive in the Jig sector at 12:00 hours.
▼

Throughout the Battle of Normandy, flat-hulled ships grounded directly on the beach to unload their cargo, hence saving considerable time for

07:30 Fierce combat at La Rivière for the East Yorkshires

The 69th Brigade's other battalion, the 5th East Yorkshire, landed at La Rivière, at the eastern extremity of Gold Beach. WN33, with its formidable 88mm gun, destroyed two Sherman DD tanks, one after the other, but a third Allied tank succeeded in approaching close enough to the casemate to neutralise the German gun. Meanwhile, the infantrymen suffered heavy losses under enemy machine gunfire, survivors struggling to the sea wall for shelter with no hope of progressing any further inland. Destroyers then began to attack the German position and the East Yorkshires finally managed to overpower the WN from the rear. The first companies continued their progression southwards and at 09:30 took control of the fortification at the Mont Fleury lighthouse, taking thirty German soldiers prisoner.

The same blockhouse today.

▲ This powerful blockhouse housed an 88mm gun that was responsible for the loss of two special tanks. The position was finally destroyed by gunfire from a Sherman flail tank. *IWM A023995.*

LANDING OF THE NORTHUMBRIANS

LANDING OF REINFORCEMENTS

As from 08:15, reinforcement units began to land. In the Jig sector, the 2nd Devons arrived under streams of enemy fire from Le Hamel, but they joined forces with the Hampshires and finally succeeded in weakening the position. They were shortly followed by the 47th RM Commando which lost four of its fourteen landing barges before they even reached the beach. Lieutenant-Colonel Phillips' men were then delayed by the resulting chaos that hampered progression on the beach. They neutralised a few groups of German troops before reaching their assembly point at the church in Le Hamel by the early afternoon.

The last of the 69th Brigade's battalions, the 7th Green Howards, landed in turn in the King sector and advanced towards the Mare-Fontaine battery which they took without resistance, its garrison still shocked by the bombardments they had already endured.

Late morning, General Graham's two other brigades were also hard at work. All of the coastal defences, with the exception of Le Hamel, had been annihilated. The British troops were free to move inland.

Along the coastline, the 1st Hampshires struggled for several hours to take control of Le Hamel. Deadly gunfire came from the sanatorium in particular. At 16:00 hours, with support from Churchill tanks, equipped with 290mm Petard mortars, the German strong point was finally put out of action, following fierce man-to-man combat.

▲ The first wounded troops were evacuated to hospital ships. On the 6th of

The incessant flow of incoming reinforcements obliged strict organisation by Royal Navy Beach Groups. This picture shows one of their command posts. Judging by the Royal Navy White Ensign flying above the post, the 6th of June was a windy day. *Cliché IWM A024092.*

Commodore Douglas Pennant, Naval Commander of Force G, talking to Engineer troops immediately after he landed from aboard HMS Bulolo. *IWM A023944.*

The Royal Engineers hard at work on Gold Beach. German defences referred to as Czech hedgehogs lined up alongside bundles of sticks to be used to fill any necessary holes. *IWM A023947.*

The battalion pursued its progression towards Arromanches. Thanks to accurate naval artillery fire, the *Hampshires* took control of the village the same evening. In turn, Lieutenant-Colonel Phillips' commandos reached Hill 72 to the south of Longues. However, their target - Port-en-Bessin - was as yet out of reach, and was only to be controlled on the 8th of June.

Further south, the South Wales Borderers advanced via La Rosière and reached the Pouligny radar station, by then dismantled by the Germans. By late afternoon, they had established a bridgehead on the River Aure near Vaux. The regiment was followed by the 2nd Essex and the 2nd Gloucester, which set up camp in Saint-Sulpice and Magny. A few patrols were even dispatched to Bayeux, although the town's liberation was postponed to the following day.

The 69th and 151st Brigades continued their progression to the south of Ver-sur-Mer. German positions were overthrown, one after another, such as the battery to the west of Crépon where Company Sergeant-Major Hollis distinguished himself (see opposite). The River Seulles was crossed, Creully was liberated and a link established with Canadian troops, when the *Kampfgruppe Meyer* entered the scene.

This monument in honour of the Green Howards can be admired not far from the spot where the company's Sergeant Hollis distinguished himself.

Rhino Ferries landing 50th Division vehicles and first 7th Armoured Division units on Gold Beach. These ferries provided a precious link between the ships out at sea and the beaches.

LANDING OF THE NORTHUMBRIANS

The first 7th Armoured Division units landed on Gold in the evening. A Cromwell tank led this column. The countless embarkations of all sorts and sizes that comprised the Allied armada can be seen in the background. *IWM B005251.*

▲ Men from the 50th Division advancing alongside a Caen stone wall, typical of the Bessin area.

The Victoria Cross is the British Army's most distinguished military decoration.
It was introduced by Queen Victoria in 1856 to award valour in the face of the enemy.

Company Sergeant-Major Hollis

Stanley Hollis was a Company Sergeant-Major in the 6th Green Howards' D Company. He landed at Hable de Heurtot with the first waves of assault. After having neutralised strong point WN35, his unit headed for the Mont Fleury artillery battery. Hollis was to distinguish himself, first and foremost, on the perimeter of this defensive position. With his Sten submachine gun and a few grenades, he neutralised a first bunker before heading, via a trench, for a second, where the garrison surrendered. He was later entrusted with the mission of destroying an armed position to the west of Crépon, on his company's approach to the village. He planned to use a PIAT rocket launcher which, at the fateful moment, failed to fire. However, he finally managed to take control of the guns and to destroy them. He then created a diversion to reach two men who had found themselves surrounded. For all of these feats of arms, he was the only British soldier on D-Day to be decorated with the Victoria Cross, the highest distinction in the British Army.

THE GERMAN REACTION

In the first hours of the landings, the German defences were rapidly crushed, with the exception of Omaha Beach, where the men from General Kraiss' *352.Infanterie- Division* boldly resisted the American landings. However, when Kraiss was informed that British troops had reached the Meuvaines crest in the Gold Beach sector, he feared his right flank in danger of encirclement. He consequently asked his superior General Marcks, commander of the *84.Korps*, to send his only available reserve to counter the Allied threat. Part of the 915th Regiment then received orders to assemble in the Villiers-le-Sec sector and to counter-attack towards Crépon. This *Kampfgruppe* (combat group), commanded by Colonel Meyer, comprised a battalion from the 915th Regiment, the 352nd Fusilier Battalion and ten self-propelled guns belonging to the 1352nd Assault Gun Company. Meyer also brought in withdrawn troops to reinforce his group.

At 11:00 hours, the German units started their advance under incessant fire from Allied fighter-bombers ; they consequently only reached their target position at 16:00 hours. Barely had Meyer reassembled his troops when he was challenged by units from the 69th Brigade. The opening engagements were in favour of the Germans and four Sherman DDs were put out of action. However, his *Kampfgruppe* was quick to lose its group cohesion. Meyer was killed in the action that followed and only ninety survivors retreated to Ducy-Sainte-Margeurite during the night. The only counter-attack in the Gold Beach sector was nevertheless to be a long one. The Germans had very few remaining resources to defy the British troops.

By the evening of the 6th of June, twenty-five thousand men had landed on Gold Beach, four hundred and thirteen of whom were killed, lost or wounded (ten times less than on Omaha Beach). Although Bayeux had not yet been liberated and the link with the American troops from Omaha was yet to be established, General Graham's men had nevertheless formed a solid bridgehead. The first units from the 7th Armoured Division landed in the evening to reinforce the position.

Late afternoon, men from the 1st Hampshires who had landed in Asnelles finally reached Arromanches. The seafront village was only totally cleared in the evening.

Bayeux was liberated the following day by units from the 2nd Essex. The 50th Northumbrian Division then advanced southwards to Tilly-sur-Seulles where it was finally stopped in its tracks by the Panzer-Lehr, General Bayerlein's elite armoured unit. The division fought valiantly to secure Lingèvres on the 12th of June, followed by Tilly on the 18th. From then on, all attempts to move further inland were in vain and every foot of progression was at a cost of heavy losses. The Allied advance was only to resume in August, after the germans had retreated around the Dives and the Seine

▲After the coastal defences had been neutralised, German resistance weakened and the British troops could advance to the outskirts of Bayeux on the very evening of the 6th of June. The first prisoners were sent to the beaches to board for England.

MULBERRIES ON THE NORMANDY COASTLINE

The successful landings on the 6th of June often led to believe that the entire operation Overlord was also ordained to meet with success. Yet the truly critical phase for the Allies only began the day after D-Day. It consisted in supplying, reinforcing and consolidating the bridgehead before the Germans could organise a powerful counter-attack. The overall success of Overlord consequently relied on the Allies' capacity to implement an effective logistic strategy. Furthermore, they were at a disadvantage compared to the Germans for they needed to bring their reinforcements from across the Channel. The Air Force, together with the deception operation, co-denamed *Fortitude*, were nevertheless to compensate for their relative weakness by bombing the enemy advance routes or by deluding the Germans into believing that a further landing was planned for the Pas-de-Calais region.

Construction of Phoenix caissons. A total of 212 were built in the Thames estuary and in Southampton.

Yet, the implementation of adequate logistic capacities remained a crucial challenge. For example, an American division consumed some one thousand six hundred tonnes of supplies every day. The control of a harbour was the only way to meet such a challenge. However, Hitler had fortified them all. A direct attack on one of these fortresses was therefore not an option; the bloody experience of Dieppe offered bitter proof. Based on work by the engineer Guy Maunsell and upon advice from Commodore Hugues-Hallet, Admiral Mountbatten put forward the idea to build a prefabricated harbour and to ship its various elements across the English Channel before reassembling them in Normandy.

DESIGNING ARTIFICIAL HARBOURS

As soon as he got wind of these artificial harbour projects, Churchill immediately and utterly defended them. The first tests were conducted in 1943 and construction began in October. Forty-five thousand labourers were actively involved in the construction of the various elements that would combine to form two artificial harbours. The first Mulberry, «A» for American, was to be established off Saint-Laurent-sur-Mer on Omaha Beach and the second, «B» for British, was to be built off Arromanches.

The artificial harbour in Arromanches was operational as from the 14th of June. The breakwater formed by the Phoenix caissons and old sunken ships can clearly be seen, as well as the docks that were linked to the shore by floating causeways.

The harbours' first constituents were built in Portland: breakwaters measuring two hundred by twenty-five feet, referred to as *Bombardons* and aimed at offering the first protection from the elements. They were to be moored in the high seas, off the coast. The harbour itself was formed of a sea wall comprising Phoenix caissons and seventeen old ships, referred to as blockships, which were ballasted with concrete. Phoenix caissons are huge blocks of concrete with compartments; they were towed across the English Channel then filled with water to ensure they rested on the sea bed. Six models of varying sizes were developed, taking into account the different water levels from the high seas to the shoreline. They were built in the Thames estuary and in Southampton.

The fact that a second harbour was built opposite Omaha Beach is often forgotten: Mulberry A. It was operational as from the 17th of June, but was completely destroyed by the storm that raged from the 19th to the 22nd.

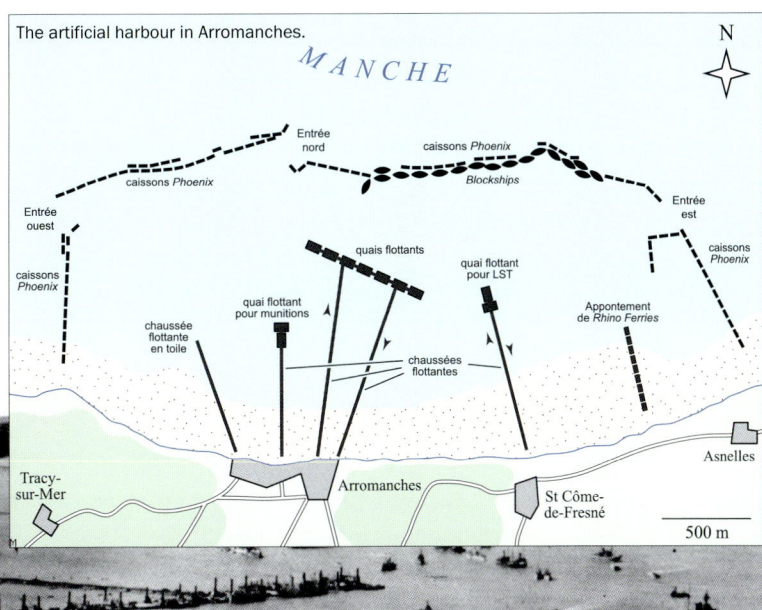

The artificial harbour in Arromanches.

In this five hundred hectare artificial harbour, 1,000m^2 (1,200 sq. yard) platforms, referred to as Loebnitz served as docks. The particularity of these platforms lay in the fact that they moved in time with the flow and ebb of the tide, sliding up and down four stakes that were solidly attached to the sea bed. Floating roadways were attached to these docks, enabling both men and vehicles to reach the shore, independently of the water level.

In just eight months, a total of two hundred and twelve Phoenix caissons, twenty-three platforms and over nine miles of floating roadways were built. The first elements were towed simultaneously to the deployment of Force G ships.

A Loebnitz platform being installed. The stakes on its four corners were placed on the sea bed. The platform then slid up and down these stakes in time with the tide. Boats could subsequently unload throughout the day.

▲ GMCs on a Loebnitz platform on their way to the floating causeways that would take them to shore.

PORT WINSTON

Barely had they landed, the engineers set to work in Saint-Laurent and Arromanches. The first elements arrived on the Normandy coast as early as the 7th of June and construction began immediately. It was scheduled to last three months. Yet the first ships berthed as early as the 14th of June. Over the following days, increasing supplies were unloaded, while both harbours were struck by a violent storm from the 19th to the 22nd of June. The American harbour which, contrary to Arromanches, was not supported by a rocky sea bed, suffered excessive damage and was abandoned. Mulberry B had proved more resistant to the elements and was repaired. It was soon to reach a daily flow of seven thousand tonnes of supplies.

Vehicles could reach dry land thanks to floating docks. Four routes were built in Arromanches, two of which were one-way: one outbound and one inbound. *IWM A024360.*

▲ Thanks to flat-hulled vessels, men, material and vehicles could be landed directly on the beach. This technique was to offer results that largely surpassed Allied expectations. They succeeded in landing more material on a beach such as Omaha

The harbour benefited from the utmost protection against aerial attack. Several Phoenix caissons were equipped with turrets housing anti-aircraft guns. A system of artificial fog was also used. Finally, barrage balloons prevented German planes from approaching for they risked hitting the cables that held them in place.

The artificial harbour in Arromanches was for a long time considered to be one of the essential ingredients in the Allied success. It was soon to be baptised Port Winston in honour of the decisive role played by Churchill who was the driving force behind its construction. In recent years, historians have tended to minimise the harbour's importance. It is of note that the Allies, very shrewdly, did not concentrate their entire logistic effort on artificial harbours. As soon as they were liberated, the small harbour towns along the coast, such as Port-en-Bessin, Courseulles, Grandcamp and Isigny were restored and adapted to receive around a thousand tonnes of supplies every day. But it was the quantities unloaded directly on the beaches that were to largely surpass Allied estimations. When the various elements that comprised the artificial harbours were assembled, old ships were also scuttled in the high seas off each beach, forming five Gooseberries.

▲ The harbour in Arromanches was protected by a range of defensive systems: anti-aircraft guns installed on top of the Phoenix caissons, artificial fog and barrage balloons to prevent German planes from flying above.

Sheltered by these breakwaters, a fleet of LSTs (flat-based vessels equipped with bow doors and capable of grounding on the beach), DUKWs (amphibious trucks) and *Rhino Ferries* (barges) unloaded equipment and troops directly onto the sand. By late June, Omaha, Juno and Gold respectively unloaded 13,000, 5,200 and 4,500 tonnes. Ultimately, 48 % of British supplies were transported via Arromanches, i.e. 25% of total Allied supplies.

Hence, even if Port Winston was not the Allies' unique logistic tool, it was nevertheless one of the essential links in logistic manoeuvres. It continued to be used well after the end of the Battle of Normandy and was only closed when the Allies took hold of Antwerp in November 1944.

Arromanches harbour is one of the sites not to be missed when touring the D-Day Landing beaches. On the beach, the vestiges of a link used to connect the platforms to beetles, the floating elements that maintained the causeways in place. Offshore, the Phoenix caissons continue to this very day to withstand the elements.

GOLD BEACH, TODAY

Gold Beach today.

Arromanches 360 plunges visitors into the story of the Battle of Normandy, thanks to archive footage projected on a 360° screen.

Today, in the former Gold Beach sector, many vestiges still bear witness to the landing of the British troops from the 50th Northumbrian. On the beach itself, several bunkers can still be seen, their only remaining assailant being the sea spray. The most worthy of note are located in La Rivière at Ver-sur-Mer and in Le Hamel at Asnelles. The vestiges of the artificial harbour in Arromanches comprise one of France's most remarkable heritage sites. Several Phoenix caissons and even a few beetles, the elements that supported the floating roadways, can still be admired today. A few miles westwards, the artillery battery in Longues-sur-Mer has been remarkably preserved with its four casemates and its firing command post.The site was even used for the legendary film The Longest Day.

Several museums have been developed along the coast, each of them covering its own theme. The D-Day Museum in Arromanches offers an educational presentation of how the artificial harbour was operated. Arromanches 360 in turn offers a journey through the Battle of Normandy via several archives projected on a 360° cinema screen. The Shipwreck Museum in Port-en-Bessin presents the multitude of items collected

▲ The D-Day Museum in Arromanches specifically focuses on the construction of the artificial harbour. Matthieu Barrabé – www.airstudio.fr